# West Coast Recreational Fisheries for Salmon

by

P. M. Washington
Fishery Research Biologist

## INTRODUCTION

Recreational or sport fisheries for Pacific salmon (genus <u>Oncorhynchus</u>) are conducted along the west coast of North America from central California north to Alaska's Arctic region. Salmon angling along the West Coast has increased in magnitude and stature since the early 1880's. The sport has grown from a few trollers off Monterey, California, to over 4 million angler days of effort annually in Washington-Oregon alone. Native Americans (Indians) were the first to capture Pacific salmon. Frank Haw and Ray Buckley (1972) theorize that there had to be some pleasure derived from the struggle. However, from what is known of the importance of the salmon to the pre-European Indian economy and the attendant ceremony, one could equally surmise that the harvest of salmon was strictly business.

Puget Sound, Washington, being unique as a large body of protected salt water on the Pacific Coast, has been a center of salmon angling activity. Most of the techniques and strategies used by West Coast recreational fishermen were developed there. From trolling with spoons in the 1880's, some enterprising anglers developed techniques for fishing with Pacific herring, <u>Clupea harengus pallas</u>, from piers by 1910. Boathouses played a major role in "Sound" salmon fishing--from the 1930's through the 1950's--providing rental boats to anglers and the forum and atmosphere in which the "angler macho" could be displayed or talked about. Prior to World War II, sport angling in Puget

Sound was largely in proximity to metropolitan centers--Elliott and Shilshole Bays in Seattle, Port Gardner in Everett, and Commencement Bay in Tacoma. Along with the advent of lightweight metal and synthetic boat building materials in the 1950's came a period of unprecedented prosperity. The 150 boathouses on Puget Sound soon gave way to the fleet of privately-owned power boats.

Coastal ports established earlier in the century by commercial fishing fleets also underwent a transition during the 1950's. At such well-known ports as Westport, Willapa Harbor, Ilwaco, and LaPush in Washington (not to mention Coos , Depoe, and Winchester Bays in Oregon)--sport salmon angling had been almost non-existent before 1950. The sport fishery in all these ports metamorphosed from a few "locals" fishing "inside" in the coastal bays and estuaries with skiffs, to fleets of large, fast, deep-sea charter boats. During this period, improvements of services, of launching and moorage facilities, and of pleasure boats resulted in a sport fishery that is today a vital industry.

Salmon derbies have played a major role in the growth of salmon fisheries. A salmon fishing derby is, in general, a contest in which a prize is given to the contestant catching the largest salmon. Over the years, salmon derbies have been as much a part of summer as corn is a part of Iowa. Famous derbies include the Port Angeles Derby; Poggie Club Derby in Westport, Washington; Vancouver, B.C., Canada Derby; Golden North Derby in Juneau, Alaska; and, recently, the Seattle Seafair Derby. Prizes range from a few dollars to cars, real estate, or thousands of dollars.

In recent years, a freshwater fishery for salmon has sprung up in Washington, due for the most part to major changes in management philosophy by the State Department of Fisheries. As a result of these changes, Washington now offers some fine spring, summer, and fall river fishing.

The trend in sport fishery catches of salmon along the West Coast from Alaska to California has either leveled off or begun to drop (Figure 1). Washington State still leads in amounts caught as well as number of sport fishermen (almost 500,000 anglers), with a marine angling effort of 1.5 million angler days in 1970 (Table 1). Figure 2 gives a comparative view of the West Coast commercial troll fishery.

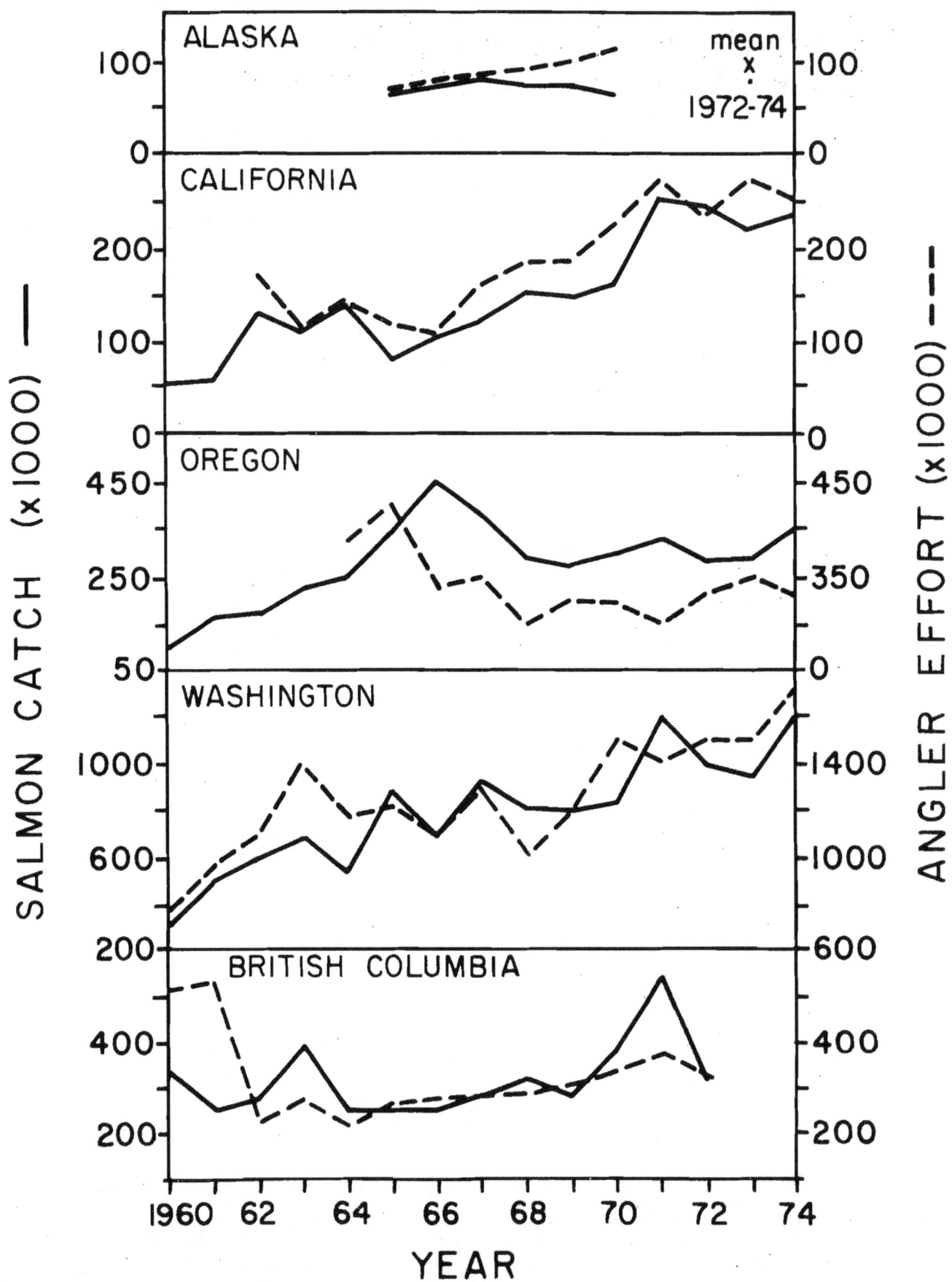

Figure 1.--West coast sport salmon fishery catch and effort (angler trips) data (1960-1974).

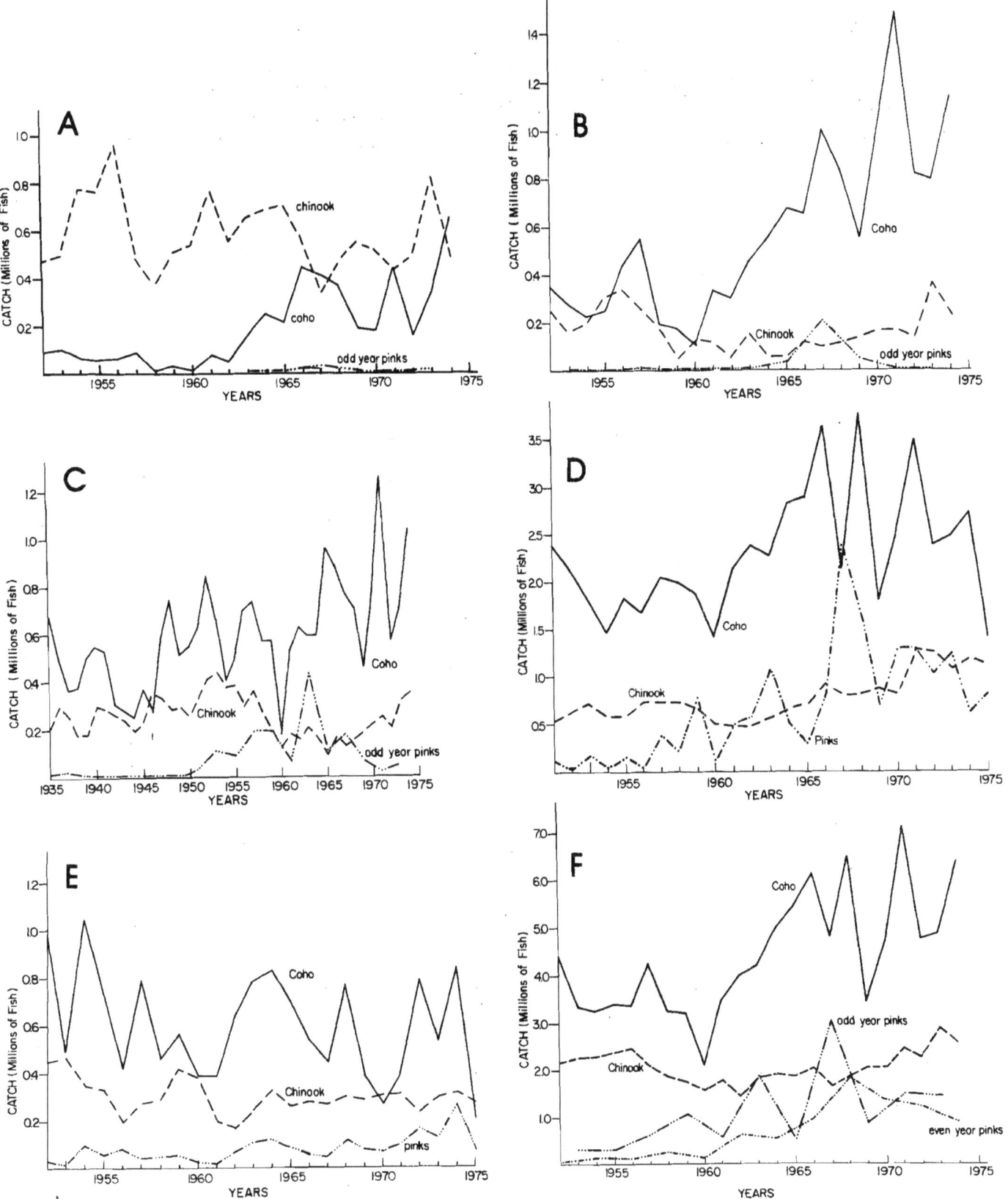

Figure 2.—Commercial salmon troll catches for (A) California, (B) Oregon,
(C) Washington, (D) British Columbia, (E) Southeastern Alaska, and
(F) all areas combined, 1952-1975 (National Marine Fisheries Service,
1977[1]).

1/ National Marine Fisheries Service, 1977.  Final; environmental impact
statement/preliminary fishery management plan; troll salmon fishery
of the Pacific Coast.  Natl. Mar. Fish. Serv., NOAA, Seattle, Wash.,
128 p.

Table 1.--Marine sport salmon catch by species and state or province, 1971 (in thousands).

| Species | Washington | Oregon | California | Alaska | British Columbia |
|---|---|---|---|---|---|
| Chinook | 313.4 | 11.0 | 188.3 | 14.3 | 122.6 |
| Coho | 845.7 | 228.0 | 67.5 | 50.5 | 371.1 |
| Pink | 39.5 | -- | -- | 11.7 | 46.0 |
| Sockeye* | 20.0 | -- | -- | 22.3 | 0.2 |
| Chum | -- | -- | -- | -- | -- |

* Freshwater fishery

Washington, Alaska, and British Columbia sport catches of chinook and coho are roughly the equivalent of those area's troll landings by commercial fishermen. However, in California and Oregon troll landings are 3-5 times greater than the sport catch (Figs. 1 and 2).

# SALMON ANGLING EFFORT

Along the West Coast, salmon fishing is a year-round sport, limited during winter and spring only by the availability of feeding salmon (mainly coho, O. kisutch, and blackmouth--an immature chinook salmon, O. tshawytscha), and sheltered waters. Winter fisheries are pretty much confined to areas like Washington State's Puget Sound and Strait of Juan de Fuca, the Columbia River and its tributaries, and some coastal streams and their estuaries. In California, San Francisco Bay, Crescent Bay, Santa Cruz, and the Sacramento and Feather Rivers provide notable winter fisheries for salmon. In Puget Sound and the Strait of Juan de Fuca, winter salmon fisheries are generally for blackmouth. While effort is not as heavy as during the summer and fall, it is no less considerable (and growing). To the south, river and estuarine salmon fisheries are mainly for spring chinook with the Columbia System and the Sacramento System/San Francisco Bay being primary centers of activity. These spring runs traditionally support large sport fisheries. The winter fisheries generally build in run size and effort through the spring, trailing off in May in northern California as water temperatures increase. Washington coastal sport fisheries open in mid-April (May 1 in 1976) and build through summer as maturing chinook and coho salmon (and pink salmon in odd numbered years) move onshore. Salmon have helped make Washington's coastal charter fleet one of the largest in North America.

As the maturing salmon move onshore in mid-summer, sport fisheries along the Strait of Juan de Fuca, in Puget Sound, and off the mouth of the Columbia River pick up the tempo. While places like Neah Bay, Sekiu, and Pillar Point are great producers, for the amount of angling effort expended, catch per-unit-effort tends to drop as salmon approach natal streams in Puget Sound

and the Columbia drainage. It can be generalized that the farther south one
goes in the range of the various species of Pacific salmon, the later in
the year the run. Notable exceptions are pink salmon and Skagit River/Lake
Washington sockeye salmon, O. nerka. The pink salmon in Washington State,
being a mid- to late summer fishery, attracted considerable attention in
both salt and fresh water in those odd years when escapement was sufficient
to allow a fishery.

Lake Washington sockeye salmon have been eagerly sought in fresh water
from mid-June through August by hordes of trolling anglers in years when
run size has been large enough.

When Washington and Oregon coastal fisheries "fold the tent in the fall,"
Washington still has saltwater angling in "the Strait" and the "Sound" for
coho salmon, as does Oregon in its estuaries. Salmon are pursued up most
rivers in both states by anglers until the onset of maturity strips the salmon
of its appeal.

While stream angling fisheries compete with hunting during the fall
for the sportsman, participation is still growing.

Alaska's salmon fisheries are primarily late spring and summer fisher-
ies--both marine and freshwater. Effort grows annually as access problems
are overcome. Fisheries are generally near towns, logging camps, or fish
camps.

California's salmon fisheries are fall, winter, and early spring fisheries of considerable effort.

Canada's coastal fisheries are receiving a lot more interest of late
as once inaccessible hot spots are being thrown open for the not insignificant
price of airfare, lodging, and boat rental.

# FISHING AREAS, FACILITIES, TIMES, AND PLACES

Of great interest to the angler planning an outing to any area is information on what to expect in terms of lodging, boat launching, boat rental, restaurants, etc. In general, these facilities and services have grown with the area's fisheries. Below is an attempt to break down facilities and services by state and area.

## CALIFORNIA

California's marine sport salmon fisheries are easily categorized into charter boat and skiff categories. The California coast is not subject to the same winter conditions found along the coast of the more northern states. As a result, coastal fishing occurs from mid-February to December.

With the exception of San Francisco Bay, most California ports are more or less protected coves or river estuaries. Boat launching facilities, rental skiffs, and/or charter boat services are to be found in all of these harbors.

California does not have the seasonal access-to-the-sea problems of Oregon. During the coastal season between April and December, a considerable amount of angling effort is expended by both skiff and charter boat anglers. Salmon runs to California rivers occur generally during the fall, winter, and spring months. The seasonal angling effort in rivers can again be described as considerable.

California's salmon producing areas are listed in Table 2 along with information on fishery timing, speciation, and some pertinent remarks.

## OREGON

Oregon's marine salmon fisheries are based out of coastal ports. Since, without exception, leaving and entering these ports is made hazardous by

Table 2.—Timing and site of California marine sport salmon fisheries (from Squire 1964).

| Angling site | Species taken | | | | | | | Season | | | | Time | Remarks |
|---|---|---|---|---|---|---|---|---|---|---|---|---|---|
| | Chinook | | Coho | | Pink | Sockeye | Chum | Winter | Spring | Summer | Fall | | |
| | I | M | I | M | | | | | | | | | |
| Crescent City | | x | | x | | | | | | x | x | | |
| Trinidad Head | | x | | x | | | | | | x | x | | |
| Humboldt Bay | x | x | | x | | | | | | x | x | | |
| Fort Bragg | | x | | x | | | | | x | x | x | | Fishery offshore. |
| Bodega Bay | x | x | | x | | | | | x | x | x | | |
| Point Reyes to Point San Pedro | x | x | | x | | | | | x | x | x | | Fishery extends offshore to Farallon Islands. |
| San Francisco Bay | | x | | x | | | | x | x | x | x | | Fishing better outside. |
| Santa Cruz | | | | x | | | | x | x | x | x | | |
| Sea Cliff Beach | | x | | | | | | x | x | x | x | | |
| Pacific Grove | | x | | x | | | | x | x | x | x | | Salmon migratory. Fishing good some years. Range over entire bay. Found in isolated spots. |
| Monterey Bay | x | x | | x | | | | x | | x | x | | |
| Estero Bay | | x | | x | | | | | x | x | | | |
| San Luis Obispo Bay | | x | | x | | | | | x | | | | |

a bar crossing, the major fisheries for salmon in Oregon occur in its many
rivers.

As stated earlier, the marine salmon fisheries occur in spring, summer,
and fall. Bar and weather conditions are the governing factors and skiffs
are especially subject to these elements. Even so, facilities for launching
skiffs are available in all of the major estuaries that provide harbors
along the Oregon coast. In addition, skiff rentals are available in most
ports and charter boat services occur in all Oregon ports.

In Oregon, salmon angling occurs during late spring and early fall
in the ocean and the Columbia River (and its tributaries) or during the
fall, winter, or spring in coastal rivers. Coastal sport fishery effort
is much less than in Washington and California due to limited access and
the dangers associated with navigating coastal waters at the mouths of rivers
and river estuaries. These are possibly the reasons river angling enjoys
greater popularity in Oregon. Oregon salmon hot spots are detailed in Table
3 along with information on fishery timing, species encountered, and pertinent
remarks. It should be reiterated that the range of pink, O. gorbuscha, and
sockeye salmon does not extend south of the Columbia River, and chum salmon,
O. keta, are few in number to the end of their range in the Sacramento River.

WASHINGTON

Washington marine waters can be viewed in terms of south, central,
and north Puget Sound, Hood Canal, Strait of Juan de Fuca, and coast. Puget
Sound and Hood Canal have, in general, "private skiff" fisheries. Boat rentals are available, as are charter services, but the major proportion of
services and facilities are aimed at the private boat owner. Marinas, both
private and public, are common and provide for boat launching (ramp and/or

Table 2.—Timing and site of California marine sport salmon fisheries (from Squire 1964).

| Angling site | Chinook I | Chinook M | Coho I | Coho M | Pink | Sockeye | Chum | Winter | Spring | Summer | Fall | Time | Remarks |
|---|---|---|---|---|---|---|---|---|---|---|---|---|---|
| Crescent City | | x | | x | | | | | x | x | | | |
| Trinidad Head | | x | | x | | | | | x | x | | | |
| Humboldt Bay | | x | x | x | | | | | x | x | | | |
| Fort Bragg | | x | | x | | | | | x | x | x | | Fishery offshore. |
| Bodega Bay | x | | | x | | | | | x | x | x | | |
| Point Reyes to Point San Pedro | x | x | | x | | | | | x | x | x | | Fishery extends offshore to Farallon Islands. |
| San Francisco Bay | | x | | | | | | x | x | x | x | | Fishing better outside. |
| Santa Cruz | | | x | | | | | x | x | x | x | | Salmon migratory. Fishing good some years. Range over entire bay. Found in isolated spots. |
| Sea Cliff Beach | | x | | | | | | x | x | x | x | | |
| Pacific Grove | | x | | x | | | | x | x | x | x | | |
| Monterey Bay | | x | | x | | | | x | x | x | x | | |
| Estero Bay | | | x | | | | | | x | x | | | |
| San Luis Obispo Bay | | | x | | | | | | x | x | | | |

Table 3.—Timing and site of Oregon marine sport salmon fisheries (from Squire 1964).

| Angling site | Chinook I | Chinook M | Coho I | Coho M | Pink | Sockeye | Chum | Winter | Spring | Summer | Fall | Time | Remarks |
|---|---|---|---|---|---|---|---|---|---|---|---|---|---|
| Chitco Cove | x | x | x | | | | | | x | x | | | |
| Brookings Gold Beach | | x | | | | | | | x | x | | | Offshore fishery developing. |
| Coos Bay | | x | x | | | | | | x | x | x | | Fishery offshore and in bay. |
| Winchester Bay | | x | x | | | | | | x | x | x | | Fall chinook major run. Bar hazardous. Fishing on bar and outside when conditions are right. |
| Newport | | x | x | | | | | | x | x | x | | Offshore fishery. |
| Yaquina Bay | | x | x | | | | | | x | x | x | | |
| Depoe Bay | | x | x | | | | | | x | x | x | | Offshore fishery. |
| Nestucca Bay | | x | x | | | | | | x | x | | | Fishery in bay and offshore. |
| Tillamook Bay | | x | | x | | | | | x | x | x | | "   "   "   "   " |

hoist), marine gas, bait, and services. Generally lodging is close at hand, at or near resorts in outlying areas, or near marinas in more heavily popu- lated areas.

The importance of the resort to the angler increases as one travels west on the Strait of Juan de Fuca. In general, resorts along the strait offer all of the facilities and services the sport angler could require. While use of private skiffs still predominates, rental boats and charter boats play an increasing role as one approaches the coast. This is possibly a function of the distance from the population centers and the expense of trailering a skiff from those centers.

Washington's coastal sport fishery is primarily a charter boat fishery. However, ever-increasing numbers of private skiffs fish out of the four coastal ports, and facilities and services have expanded accordingly. It should be mentioned that, while available lodging can't hope to cope with the number of anglers that flock to "outer" strait and coastal fishing ports, facilities for campers and trailers have adequately filled the void. The major portion of the angling effort is during the summer months; however, substantial fisheries exist during all seaons, varying by locality (Table 4).

BRITISH COLUMBIA

The remoteness of the islands and north coast areas of British Columbia is no doubt the major limiting factor in angling effort. However, sport angling along the southern mainland coast and along the Vancouver Island coast is extensive and productive during most of the year.

In Table 5 is a list of productive British Columbia salmon angling areas and the timing, species available, and other pertinent information.

Table 4a.--Timing and site of Washington marine salmon angling[1]

| Angling site | Chinook | | Coho | | Pink | Sockeye | Chum | Winter | Spring | Summer | Fall | Time | Remarks |
|---|---|---|---|---|---|---|---|---|---|---|---|---|---|
| | I | M | I | M | | | | | | | | | |
| **South Puget Sound** | | | | | | | | | | | | | |
| Dougel Point | x | | | | | | | x | x | | | | Dogfish problems |
| Steam Boat Island | x | | | | | | | x | x | | | Early AM & tide changes | Dogfish abundant |
| Cooper Point | x | | | | | | | x | x | | | | Dogfish abundant |
| Johnson Point | x | | | | | | | | x | x | | Tide changes | Fish west side of Point during late stages of flood and SE of Point during ebb |
| Devils Head | x | | | | | | | x | x | | | | |
| Anderson Island | x | x | | x | | | x | x | x | x | x | | Ebb tides best producers from late fall through winter and flood tides best during warmer months |
| Eagle Island | x | | | | | | | x | x | | | | |
| Toliva Shoal | x | | x | | x | | | | x | | | Flood tides | |
| Gibson-Fox Point | x | x | | | | | | x | x | x | x | | |
| Wollochit Bay | x | | x | | | | | x | x | x | x | | Chinook fishing best in Dec. Dogfish |
| Green Point (Sandspit) | x | | x | | | | | x | x | x | x | | |
| "Gallagan's Head" | x | | | | | | | x | x | x | x | | |
| Raft/Cutts I. | x | | | | | | | x | | | | | "Dap" slot along NW side of islands a good producer |
| Minter Creek | | x | | x | | | | | | x | x | Early AM | |
| Purdy | x | | | | | | | x | x | | x | Flood tides early AM late PM | |
| Point Evans | x | | | | | | | x | | | | Ebb tide | |
| **Central Sound** | | | | | | | | | | | | | |
| Point Defiance | x | x | x | | | | | | x | x | | Tide change | |
| Point Dalco | x | | | | | | | | | | | Flood tides | |
| Quartermaster Hbr | x | | | | | | | x | | | x | | |
| Commencement Bay/ Browns Point | | | | | | | | | | | | | |
| Redondo | x | | x | x | | | | x | | x | | | |
| Point Richmond | | | | | | | | | | | | | |
| Camp Sealth | x | | | | | | | x | | | | Tide Rips | |
| Allen Bank | x | | | | | | | x | x | | | | |
| Orchard Point | x | | | | | | | x | | | | | |
| Bainbridge Reef | | x | | | | | | | | x | | | |
| Port Orchard | x | | | | | | | x | | | x | | |
| Dyes Inlet | x | | | | | | | x | | | x | | |
| Elliott Bay | x | x | x | | | | | x | x | x | | | |
| Skiff Point | x | | | | | | | x | | | x | | |
| Shilshole Point | x | x | x | | | | | x | x | x | x | | |
| Point Monroe | x | | | | | | | x | | | x | | |
| Agate Pass | x | | | | | | | | x | x | | | |
| Jefferson Head | x | x | x | x | | | | x | x | x | x | | |
| "The Trees" | x | x | | | | | | x | x | x | x | | |
| Point Wells to Edmonds | x | | | | | | | x | | | | | |
| Possession Bar | x | x | x | x | x | | | | | | | Early AM | |
| Lake Washington[2] | | x | | x | | x | | | | x | x | | |
| Meadowdale to Mukilteo | x | x | x | x | | | | x | | x | | Early AM | |
| Glendale to Columbia Beach | | x | x | x | | | | | | x | | | |
| Mission Bar/ Port Gardner | x | x | x | x | | | | x | | x | x | | |
| Point No Point | x | x | x | | | | | x | x | x | x | Ebb tides | |
| Skunk Bay | x | | | | | | | x | x | | | | |
| Double Bluff | x | | x | | | | | | x | x | | Ebb tides | Not as productive in recent years |
| Foulweather Bluff | x | | x | | | | | | x | x | | | Fish tide rips |
| Gedney (Hat) I. | x | x | x | x | | | | | | x | | | Most consistent off north and for coho |
| Sandy Point | x | | | | | | | | | x | | | |
| Pebble Beach Coves | x | | | | | | | x | | | | | |
| Spit | | | | | | | | | | | | | |
| East Point ("foxes Spit") | x | | | | | | | x | x | x | x | | |
| Baley I. | x | | x | | | | | x | x | x | x | | Fish taken in shallow water |
| Dines Point | x | | | | | | | x | x | | | | |
| Helms Harbor | x | | | | | | | x | x | | | | Fish attracted by spawning herring |
| McKee Beach | x | | | | | | | x | x | | | | |
| Onamac Utsately | x | x | x | x | | | | | x | x | x | | Very good when bait fish are abundant |
| Snatelum/Forbes P. | x | | | | | | | x | | | | | |
| Polnell Point | x | x | | | | | | x | x | x | | | |

| Angling site | Chinook I | Chinook M | Coho I | Coho M | Pink | Sockeye | Chum | Winter | Spring | Summer | Fall | Time | Remarks |
|---|---|---|---|---|---|---|---|---|---|---|---|---|---|
| **Central Sound (Continued)** | | | | | | | | | | | | | |
| Oak Bay | x | x | | | | | | x | x | x | x | | |
| "Windmill Hole" | x | | | | | | | x | x | x | | Late PM | |
| Liplip Point | x | x | | | | | | | | x | | | |
| Bush Point | x | x | x | x | x | | | x | x | x | x | | |
| Lagoon Point | | | | x | x | | | | | x | x | | |
| Marrow Stone Point | x | x | | x | | | | | | x | x | | |
| Port Townsend | x | | | | | | | x | | | | | |
| Point Wilson | x | x | | x | x | | | | | x | x | | |
| Admiralty Head | x | | | x | x | | | x | | x | x | | |
| **Hood Canal** | | | | | | | | | | | | | |
| Pleasant Harbor | x | | | | | | | x | x | | | | |
| Misery Point | x | x | x | x | | | | | x | x | x | | |
| Dosewallips | | | | | x | | | | | x | | | Odd year run only |
| Tskutsko Point to Oak Head | x | | x | x | | | | x | x | x | | | |
| Dabob Bay | x | | | | | | | x | | | | | |
| Hazel Point | x | | | | | | | x | x | | | Early AM | Dogfish can be a problem |
| Hamma Hamma | x | x | | | | | | | | x | x | Early AM | |
| Lilliwaup | x | | x | | | | | | x | x | | | |
| Dewatto | | | | x | | | | | | x | x | | |
| Hoods Port | x | x | | x | | | | x | x | x | x | Early AM | |
| Indian Hole | x | x | | | | | | | x | x | | | |
| Bald Point | x | x | | | | | | | x | x | | Early Am Flood tides | |
| Union | x | x | | x | | | | | x | x | x | AM ebb tide | |
| Tahuya | | | | x | | | | | | x | x | | |
| Chicken Hole | x | | | | | | | x | | | | | |
| **San Juan Islands North Puget Sound** | | | | | | | | | | | | | |
| West Beach and Deception Pass | | x | | x | x | | | | | x | | | |
| Hope I. | | x | | | | | | | x | x | | | East end during flood/west end during ebb |
| Langley (Big) P. | x | | | | | | | x | x | | | | |
| Iceberg Point | x | | | | | | | | x | x | | | |
| Lopez Pass | x | | | | | | | x | | | | | |
| Reef Point | x | x | | x | | | | | x | x | x | | |
| Guemes Channel | x | | | | | | | x | | | | | |
| Cypress I. | x | x | | x | | | | x | x | x | x | | West side of Island |
| William Point | x | | | | | | | x | x | | | | |
| East Sound | x | | | | | | | x | | | | | Particularly good fishing near entrance |
| Point Lawrence | x | x | x | x | | | | | x | | x | | |
| Sinclare I. | x | | | | | | | | x | x | | | |
| Lummi Rocks | | x | | x | | | | | | x | | | |
| Hale Passage | x | | | | | | | x | | | | | |
| Orcas I. | x | x | | | | | | | | x | | | Along northeast shore |
| Waldron I. | | x | | x | x | | | | | x | | | |
| Mosquito Pass | x | | | x | | | | x | x | x | | | |
| Spieden Channel | x | | | | | | | x | | | | | |
| Point Roberts | x | x | x | x | x | | | | | x | | | |
| **Strait of Juan de Fuca** | | | | | | | | | | | | | |
| Middle Point | | x | | | x | | | | | x | | | |
| Cape George | x | | | x | | | | | | x | | | |
| Dallas Bank | x | x | | x | x | | | x | x | x | x | | |
| Diamond Point | x | | x | x | | | | | | x | x | | |
| Discovery Bay | x | | | | | | | x | x | | x | | Troll fishery |
| Partridge Bank | x | x | x | x | x | | | x | x | x | x | | Extremely exposed |
| Sequim Bay | x | | | | | | | x | | | | | |
| Dungeness Bay | | x | | | | | | | x | | | | |
| Dungeness Spit | x | x | | x | x | | | | | x | x | | |
| Green Point | x | x | | x | x | | | x | x | x | x | | |
| Port Angeles (Harbor) | x | | | | | | | x | | | x | | |
| Ediz Hook | | x | | x | x | | | | x | x | | Early AM | Pinks & coho in offshore rips |
| Freshwater Bay to Agate Bay | x | x | | x | x | | | x | x | x | | | Coho in offshore rips |
| Pillar Point | x | x | | x | x | | | | | | | Early AM | " " " " |
| "Coal Mine" | | x | | | | | | | | | x | " " | |
| Mussolini Rock | | x | | | | | | | | | x | " " | Big fish just outside kelp line |

| Angling site | Species taken | | | | | | | Season | | | | Time | Remarks |
|---|---|---|---|---|---|---|---|---|---|---|---|---|---|
| | Chinook | | Coho | | Pink | Sockeye | Chum | | | | | | |
| | I | M | I | M | | | | Winter | Spring | Summer | Fall | | |
| **Strait of Juan de Fuca** (Cont.) | | | | | | | | | | | | | |
| Sekiu Point to Mouth of Hoko R. | x | x | | x | x | | | x | x | x | x | Early AM | |
| Wadah I. | x | x | x | x | x | | | x | x | x | x | | |
| "Garbage Dump" | x | x | | | | | | | x | x | | Tide changes | Close in to shore |
| Midway Rocks | x | x | | | | | | | x | x | | Early AM | Just outside kelp |
| Slant Rock | x | x | | | | | | | x | x | | " " | " " " |
| **Washington Coast** | | | | | | | | | | | | | |
| Tatoosh | | x | | | | | | | x | x | | | Deepwater fishing |
| Duncan Rock | | | x | x | x | | | | | | | | Fish over broad area |
| Skagway Rocks | | x | | | | | | | x | x | | | Good shallow water fishing |
| Father & Son | | | x | | | | | | | x | | | |
| Strawberry Rock, Green Bank LaPush | x | x | x | x | x | | | | | x | x | | Easy passage to ocean on skiff |
| Grays Harbor (West Port) | x | x | x | x | | | | | x | x | x | | Featureless area - bar hazardous |
| Willapa Bay (Tokeland) | x | x | | | | | | | x | x | x | | Some fishing inside - entrance hazardous |
| Columbia River (Mouth) | x | x | x | x | | | | | | | x | | Bar hazardous - fishing over broad featureless expanse |

1/ Howard et al.(1967), and Howard Buckley 1973 Sources.

2/ Unique sockeye fishery in freshwater.

Table 5.--Timing and site of British Columbia marine sport salmon fisheries (Dept. of Fisheries of Canada 1966).

| Angling site | Species taken | | | | | | | Season | | | | Time | Remarks |
|---|---|---|---|---|---|---|---|---|---|---|---|---|---|
| | Chinook | | Coho | | Pink | Sockeye | Chum | | | | | | |
| | I | M | I | M | | | | Winter | Spring | Summer | Fall | | |
| Campbell R. | x | x | x | x | x | | | x | x | x | x | | |
| Comox-Courtenay | x | x | x | x | x | | | x. | x | x | x | | |
| Powell R. | | x | x | x | | | | x | x | x | x | | |
| Pender Harbor | | x | x | x | | | | x | x | x | x | | |
| Nanaimo | x | x | x | x | | | | x | x | x | x | | |
| Duncan-Cowichen Bay | x | x | x | x | x | | | x | x | x | x | | |
| Saanich Inlet | x | x | x | x | | | | x | x | x | x | | |
| Victoria-Sooke | x | x | x | x | x | | | x | x | x | x | | |
| Vancouver-Howe Sound | x | x | x | x | x | | | x | x | x | x | | |
| Queen Charlotte I. | | x | x | x | | | | | x | x | x | | |
| Nass River | | x | | x | | | | | x | x | x | | |
| Prince Rupert | | x | | x | | | | x | x | x | x | | |
| Kitimat | | x | | | | | | | x | x | x | | |
| Bella Bella | | x | | x | | | | | x | x | | | |
| Rivers Inlet | | x | | x | | | | | | | | | |
| Port Hardy - Alert Bay | | x | x | x | x | | | x | x | x | x | | |
| Port Alberni | | x | | x | | | | x | x | x | x | | |
| Tofino | x | x | x | x | | | | x | x | x | x | | |
| Gold and Barman Rivers | | x | x | x | | | | x | x | x | x | | |
| Kyuonot-Quatsino | x | x | x | x | | | | x | x | x | x | | |

ALASKA

Sport salmon angling facilities are limited in Alaska due to the vast-
ness of the coastal area and its sparse, widespread human habitation. As
would be expected, most of the facilities and services are centered in and
around the population centers. In some areas of southeastern Alaska, the
services of fishing cabin resorts are available. In the major coastal towns,
such as Ketchikan, Wrangell, Petersburg, Sitka, and Juneau, lodging and
launch facilities, services, and supplies are available. Charter or guide
services exist--of the above mentioned, lodging and boat rentals are said
to exist in Sitka, Petersburg, and Ketchikan. Due to the scope of the wilder-
ness encountered, fishing with a guide or charter boat is recommended where-
ever possible.

Alaska is so sparsely settled that much of the salmon resources of
recreational angling value go virtually untouched. The majority of salmon
angling effort occurs in proximity to population centers and while fishing
is mostly a late spring-summer activity, some winter salmon angling does
occur in the more populated areas of southeastern Alaska. Data and information on Alaskan fisheries are sparse and scattered, but an attempt to dissemi-
nate what is available can be found in Table 6 in terms of sites, timing,
and species available.

ANGLING TECHNIQUES

Salmon angling gear can best be dealt with by categorizing the type
of fishing or tactic. Saltwater fisheries can be categorized into mooching,
spinning, and trolling; and, while the aforementioned tactics are employed
in rivers in some cases, plunking and drift fishing are tactics fairly unique
to river angling.

Table 6.—Timing and site of Alaska marine sport salmon angling (Squire 1964).

| Angling site | Chinook I | Chinook M | Coho I | Coho M | Pink | Sockeye | Chum | Winter | Spring | Summer | Fall | Time | Remarks |
|---|---|---|---|---|---|---|---|---|---|---|---|---|---|
| **Ketchikan Area** | | | | | | | | | | | | | |
| Blanket Inlet | x | x | x | x | x | | | x | x | x | | | |
| Mountain Point | x | x | x | x | x | | | | x | x | | | |
| Naha Bay | | | | x | x | | | | x | x | | | |
| Bell I. | | x | | | | | | | x | x | | | Popular resort. |
| Yes Bay | | x | | | | | | | x | x | | | |
| Point Alewa | x | | | x | x | | | | x | x | | | |
| Point Sykes | | x | | x | x | | | | x | x | | | Guide recommended. |
| Burroughs Bay | | | | x | x | | | | x | x | | | |
| Karta Bay | | | | x | x | | | | x | x | | | |
| Chasina Point | | x | | x | x | | | | x | x | | | Use of Guide recommended. |
| Grindall I. | | x | | x | x | | | | x | x | | | " " " " |
| Vollener Point | | x | | x | x | | | | x | x | | | |
| Cramans Point | | x | | x | x | | | | x | x | | | " " " " |
| Clover | | x | | x | x | | | | x | x | | | |
| **Wrangell Area** | | | | | | | | | | | | | |
| Greys Pass | x | x | | | | | | | x | | | | |
| Wrangell Harbor | x | x | x | | | | | x | x | x | | | |
| **Petersburg Area** | | | | | | | | | | | | | |
| Cape Strait | | x | x | | | | | | | x | | | |
| Frederick Sound | x | x | x | | | | | x | x | x | | | |
| Duncan Canal- Salt Chuck | | | x | | | | | | x | x | | | |
| Security Bay | | x | x | | | | | | | x | | | |
| **Sitka Area** | | | | | | | | | | | | | |
| Sitka Sound | x | x | x | | | | | | x | x | | | Excellent fishing. |
| Port Banks | | | x | | | | | | | x | | | " " |
| **Juneau Area** | | | | | | | | | | | | | |
| Echo Cove | x | x | x | x | | | | | x | x | | | |
| North Pass | x | x | x | x | | | | | x | x | | | |
| The Breadline | x | x | x | x | | | | | x | x | | | |
| Aaron I. | x | x | x | x | | | | | x | x | | | |
| Point Retreat | x | x | x | x | | | | | x | x | | | |
| South Gultar I. | x | x | x | x | | | | | x | x | | | |
| Favorite Reef | x | x | x | x | | | | | x | x | | | |
| Barlow Cove | x | x | x | x | | | | | x | x | | | |
| Auke Bay | x | x | x | x | | | | | x | x | | | |
| Piling Point | x | x | x | x | | | | | x | x | | | |
| Outer Point | x | x | x | x | | | | | x | x | | | |
| Middle Point | x | x | x | x | | | | | x | x | | | |
| White Marker | x | x | x | x | | | | | x | x | | | |
| Point Hilda | x | x | x | x | | | | | x | x | | | |
| Dupont | x | x | x | x | | | | | x | x | | | |
| Iag Point | x | x | x | x | | | | | x | x | | | |
| Point Bishop | x | x | x | x | | | | | x | x | | | |
| Point Salisbury | x | x | x | x | | | | | x | x | | | |
| Marmion I. | x | x | x | x | | | | | x | x | | | |
| Point Arden | x | x | x | x | | | | | x | x | | | |
| Dotys Cove | x | x | x | x | | | | | x | x | | | |
| Point Gardner- "Tyee area" | x | x | x | | | | | | x | x | | | |
| **Haines/Skagway Area** | | | | | | | | | | | | | |
| Chilcoot Inlet | | x | x | x | | | | | x | x | | | |
| Taiya Inlet | | x | x | x | | | | | x | x | | | |
| **Yakutat Area** | | | | | | | | | | | | | |
| Yakutat Bay | | x | x | | | | | | | x | | | |
| **Kodiak I. Area** | | | | | | | | | | | | | |
| Monashlea Bay | | | x | | x | | | | | x | | | |
| Anton Larsen Bay | | | | | x | | | | | x | | | |
| Womens Bay | | | x | | x | | | | | x | | | |
| Middle Bay | | | x | | x | | | | | x | | | |
| Kalsin Bay | | | x | | x | | | | | x | | | |
| **Kenai Peninsula** | | | | | | | | | | | | | |
| Homer Spit | | | x | | x | | | | x | x | x | | |
| Resurrection Bay | | | x | | x | | | | x | x | x | | |
| **Norton Sound Area** | | | | | | | | | | | | | |
| Safety Lagoon | | | x | | | | | | | x | | | |

Any treatment of sport salmon angling gear would have to be placed into the proper context of tactic (i.e., mooching, spinning, trolling, casting, or plunking). Certainly a golfer wouldn't tee off with a 9 iron. Numerous types of rod and reel combinations have been perfected for the various tactics employed by serious salmon anglers from Monterey, California, northward to Norton Sound, Alaska.

A wide variety of methods is employed in salmon angling, most having had local origin in which "mother necessity" spawned an invention. A good number of the methods now used coastwide were the result of years of experimentation in the center of salmon angling--Puget Sound. Such tactics as spinning, mooching, and most of the various deep troll methods were first employed in Puget Sound. While trolling for salmon on the Pacific coast was probably done first in California's Monterey Bay, present-day tackle and methods have long been used in Washington and Puget Sound.

A highly prized game fish, salmon are most often taken by lures or baits resembling a moving or fleeing bait fish or large zooplankton. Seldom are salmon taken on an inactive bait or lure. Therefore, tactics for capturing salmon must in some way have the terminal gear moving in a manner attractive to salmon. The fishing tactics previously mentioned do just that and are meant to meet the needs of the angler under a variety of situations.

MOOCHING

Drift mooching was developed to take advantage of wind and tide as a method of causing the bait to move in a manner attractive to feeding salmon. Habits characteristic of salmon make it necessary for the mooching rod to have a sensitive tip and plenty of backbone. While a slow taper rod blank will do the job, a fast taper better facilitates setting the hook. A good rod will have enough guides to prevent line from coming into contact with the rod while the rod is arched. It is also preferable to have guides of material that are not easily cut by monofilament line—carbon steel or ceramic, for example. The handle should be of sufficient length to extend at least to the tip of the elbow, when the rod and reel are held in such a way that the thumb is on the spool.

The reel is a thing of personal preference. However, in choosing one, one should keep in mind several things, such as lightweight, yet strong; high speed of retrieve; direct drive or star drag; level wind or "thumb" guide; and "clicker" or silent feature on spool. Each serves an important function although not all reels have all of these features. Briefly, the ability of the reel to stand up under severe treatment is obvious; however, why break your arm by holding heavy gear all day? While the star drag is a nice innovation, on some reels it has a way of going on the fritz just as that brute salmon takes off on another sizzling run. In this situation I much prefer the loss of a little skin off my thumb than the loss of a good fish.

The level wind is a handy addition that keeps the line on the spool in order. Be certain to check the guide sides for wear as slight nicks in its surface can result in parted line and the loss of a fish.

The "clicker" is a handy gadget which allows the angler to leave his gear unattended in the holder. The clicker will allow the fish to take line without causing a monumental bird's nest on the reel spool while notifying the angler in sentinel fashion of the business at hand.

Line is another important consideration as it is the only thing between the angler and his quarry. This is certainly not the place to go cheap--ditto leader material. While the line should be either hard or semi-hard monofilament, the breaking strength chosen will depend on the rod "action" and tip.

Remember, while it is very easy to gain enough leverage with a heavy rod tip to part a light line, a "buggy whip" action requires some doing to part that same line. Also keep in mind when outfitting that a light line requires less weight to reach a given depth.

Mooching leader rigs are of several types which include single hook, double hook, double sliding hook, and treble hook combinations. The mooching leader is from 6 to 9 feet in length--governed by the length of the rod. Leader length serves several functions of which bait action and "angler stealth" are probably most notable.

Hooks are a very important consideration. The determination of size is based on bait size, generally, as too large a bait for the hook will "lose" the hook and too large a hook for the bait will destroy the bait.

The sliding double hook was mentioned earlier and will here be properly dealt with--R.I.P. Only the creator knows how many salmon have been lost by this "conservationists'" innovation (if the bottom hook should break off, it's all over but the shouting).

If you prefer to buy your leaders "ready made," make sure to inspect them to see that they are properly tied. All hooks, no matter how expensive, have eyes that will cut through the best of leader material. Therefore, the knot should also include a portion of the leader material through the eye to act as "chafing gear" in addition to the leader itself.

The mooching sinker is fished "fixed" or "sliding" with a split shot or rubber tubing bumper against a swivel. Mooching sinkers are generally banana-shaped leads which range from ½- to 8-ounce sizes and generally come with swivels attached to both ends. Obviously a swivel is necessary to keep the leader from wrapping up in knots with the spinning bait.

Mooching baits (Figures 3-5) are usually fresh frozen or preserved Pacific herring, Clupea harengus pallas; northern anchovy, Engraulis mordax; or "candlefish," Pacific sand lance, Ammodytes hexaptenus. While candlefish is preferred due to its toughness, herring is much more accessible and can be cut to resemble candlefish. Anchovy, on the other hand, is an attractive bait to salmon but is extremely soft. The more common methods for hooking up these baits are plug cut and whole. "Whole" is generally preferred when using frozen herring or anchovies due to their softness. In any event, some method should be used to close the mouth--paper clips work nicely.

Incidentally, when the above mentioned type gear is used in trolling, it is generally referred to as motor mooching.

Mooching is a very popular light tackle method. Mooching allows a number of people to fish effectively from a single boat using light uncomplicated gear indistinguishable from present-day spinning gear.

Mooching, like other forms of bait fishing, requires bait movement. This is accomplished by drifting with the aid of tidal currents, waves, and/or wind, or a motor or otherwise propelled boat. Points that should be made concerning relative boat speed and resultant line angles are important in that depth and bait speed are fairly species-specific. Chinook salmon generally strike a slower, deeper bait as characterized by a 40-60 degree angle of the line to water surface. Generally, chinook are associated with the bottom and seem to orient by using the bottom. Coho salmon, on the other hand, are taken on a faster, shallower bait. The line angle should be much flatter at about 20-30 degrees.

Inexperienced anglers are often seen letting out hundreds of yards of line at an extremely shallow angle in hopes of contacting bottom. The

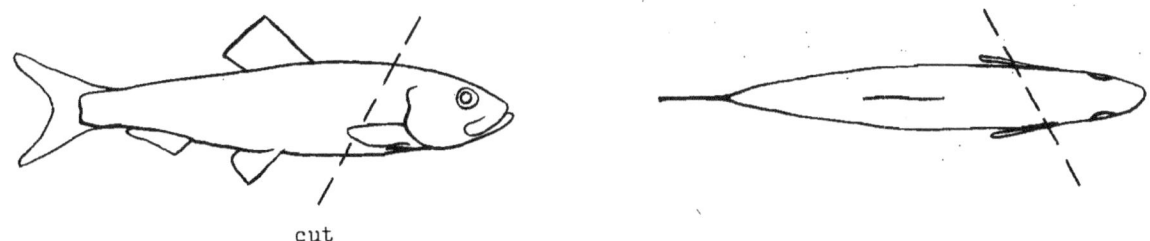

cut

Drawings show the beveled (double angle)
cut used for the cut plug bait. It is
very important to use fresh or very firm
bait as soft bait will fall apart.

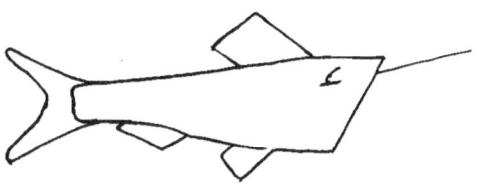

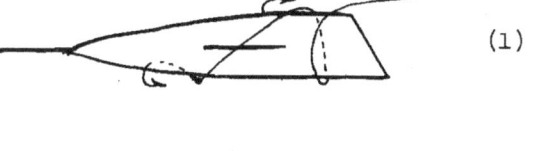

(1)

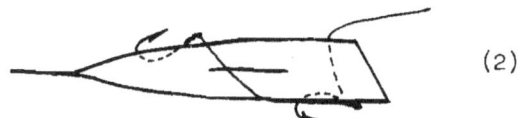

(2)

Four (4) methods of baiting a plug cut herring:
Shown are 2 hook rigs with the trailing hook
imbedded; however, the trailer can hang free
or a single hook can be used. As is the case
with the spinner cut, the speed of the roll
can be controlled by the positioning of initial
insertion of the hook--i.e. the higher the faster
the spin, the closer to center the slower. Use
of (1) gives the most secure hookup that will not
allow the bait to fall off under most circumstances
as flesh and bone are looped around by the leader
to make it secure.

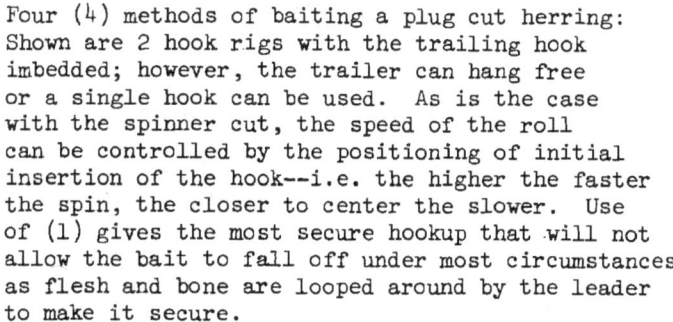

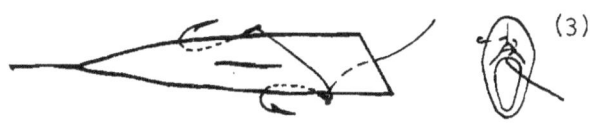

(3)

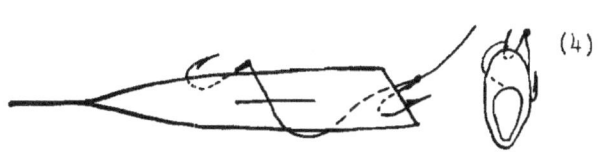

(4)

Figure 3.--The cut plug herring bait.

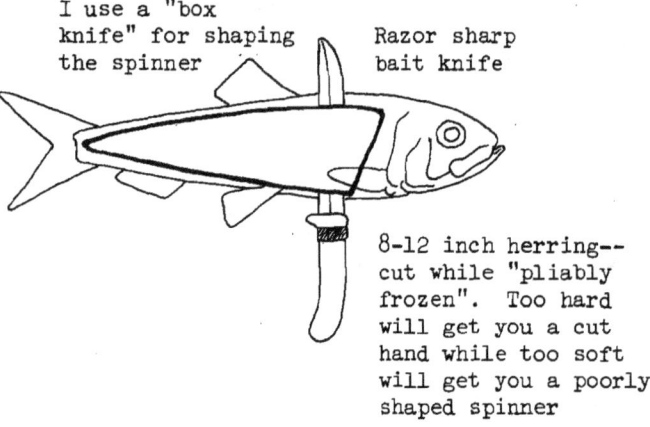

I use a "box
knife" for shaping
the spinner

Razor sharp
bait knife

8-12 inch herring--
cut while "pliably
frozen".  Too hard
will get you a cut
hand while too soft
will get you a poorly
shaped spinner

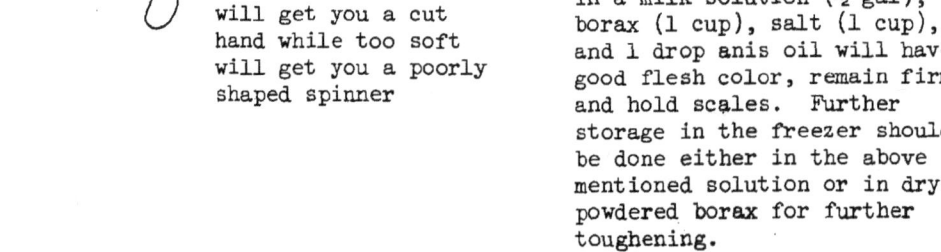

Finished "Spinner"
Be careful not to descale.
Herring that have been killed
in a milk solution (½ gal),
borax (1 cup), salt (1 cup),
and 1 drop anis oil will have
good flesh color, remain firm
and hold scales.  Further
storage in the freezer should
be done either in the above
mentioned solution or in dry
powdered borax for further
toughening.

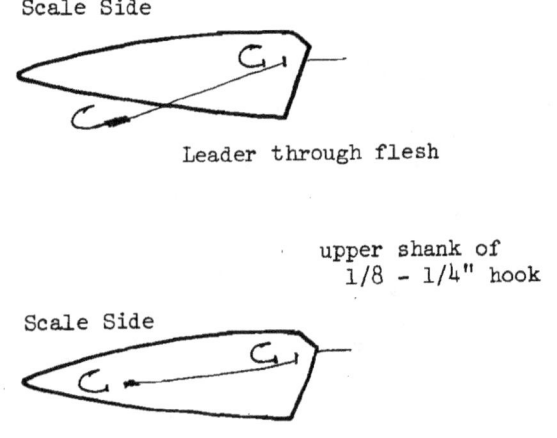

Scale Side

Leader through flesh

upper shank of
1/8 - 1/4" hook

Scale Side

Single or double hook rigs can be
used.  Vertical placement of the
forward hook will determine the
action of the spinner--the closer
to the top the faster the "spin",
the closer to the center, the slower
the "roll".  Where double hook is
used, trailer hook can be allowed
to "trail" (swing free of the bait)
or be imbedded in the rear of the
spinner.  The hooks should always
enter from the flesh side and be
pulled through.  The forward hook
is then imbedded 1/8" forward of
the initial hole so that when the
leader is snugged up a holding loop
is formed in the flesh by the leader.
HINT:  This bait is a particularly
good choice when fish are feeding
on candlefish.

Figure 4.--Cut Baits--the spinner cut herring bait.

Width of leader varies.  For salmon, use 6-7 foot
leaders

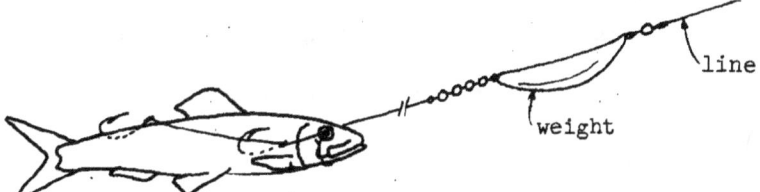

Double hook

Single hook

Termed the candlefish "harness"
rig, this method can be used on any
whole bait and is great where only
soft bait is available.  Can be
used for whole herring, candlefish,
anchovy, smelt and sardine for salmon
and marine fish.  The features of
this hookup are the loop (formed by
the hooks being passed through the eye
socket twice) which is placed under
the lower jaw to hold it closed.  The
proper bend is then formed in the bait
by cinching up on the leader while
holding the snout of the bait or while
bending its body to the desired curve.
The bait should roll in an enticing
manner.

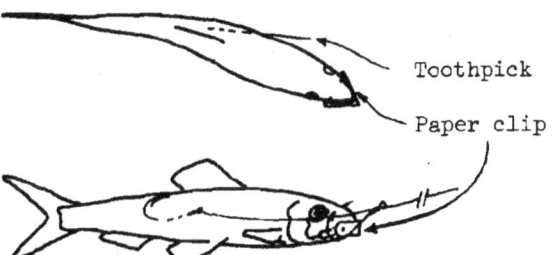

This method utilizes a toothpick to
obtain the proper body curve for
action and a paper clip to hold the
mouth of the bait closed.

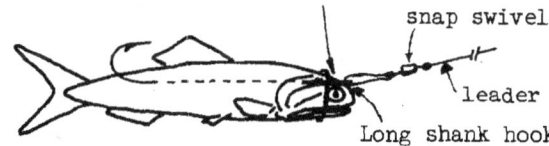

Whole anchovy rig as used in California.
Anchovies are generally a soft bait and
therefore of necessity are used whole.

Figure 5.--Whole baits.

fact is, the line drag will bring the bait closer to the surface as line out increases. Always have an idea where the bait is in relation to the water column. When line angles are not steep enough or too steep, steps should be taken that will change the angle and include changing the drift speed or changing the sinker weight.

Next to good bait in importance come cutting and baiting. Cutting a proper cut bait, be it plug or spinner cut, takes a sharp knife for a clean cut.

Howard (1947) advises the use of a single hook rig which he felt gives a better bait action. Other considerations include the fact that it is quicker to bait a single rig and there is less chance of snagging the landing net with the second hook.

While double hooks are popular, let me reiterate my dislike for the sliding hook. Eventually it is going to cost you a fish.

Double and single hook size is determined by the bait size. Generally, the leading hook is the larger hook. Haw and Buckley (1973) give a table of hook sizes.

| Finished bait length (inches) | Double hook sizes Leadhook | Trail hook | Single hook size |
|---|---|---|---|
| 3½ - 4½ | 1/0 | 1 | 1/0 |
| 4½ - 5½ | 2/0 | 1/0 | 2/0 |
| 5½ - 6½ | 3/0 | 2/0 | 3/0 |
| 6½ - 7½ | 4/0 | 3/0 | 4/0 |

As mentioned earlier, the basic tactic is to make the bait or lure look like crippled live food and it should therefore spin. While in view, the bait should be tested for its action (before casting or lowering it to the fishing depth) by pulling it through the water.

SPINNING

Spinning today means that the angler casts his bait using the same gear and bait as in drift mooching. Before the perfection of reels and line to the present state of the art, the techniques were different but again the same gears were in general use.

While spinning is and can be prosecuted from a skiff, it was developed by and for the Elliott Bay pier-bound angler.

Basically, spinning consists of casting a bait or lure out from the pier or skiff and retrieving line so as to keep the sinker and terminal gear as close to bottom as possible without contacting it.

Originally, the spinning angler would strip off a considerable amount of line and, casting with a 10- to 11- foot rod, accomplish retrieval by stripping the line in with the bait fishing just off bottom. The method soon evolved to using an anchored boat.

Modern-day spinning is hardly distinguishable from mooching which certainly had the same origins. The same gear is used in both tactics, only in spinning the skiff is anchored or drifting and bait action is due to the retrieve. Now, due mainly to advances in line materials, the cast and retrieve are directly off the reel.

Spinning is a fine light line method for capturing fish. However, it does require a little higher level of sophistication than does trolling. There are a few subtle little tricks that should be mastered. Of them, bait and tackle knowledge are the most important. Harvey Howard (1947) also mentioned that care should be used in anchoring quietly so as not to spook fish--this may or may not have a basis in fact.

Important in both mooching and spinning is knowledge about bait, and that includes obtaining and care of quality bait. Live bait is best but

is not always available and <u>good</u> frozen bait is an adequate substitute.
Not all frozen bait is good due to differences in prepackaging, handling,
and processing. The best frozen bait has been starved and is, as a result,
firm. Ragged or discolored frozen bait (bait with red cheeks and eyes, etc.)
should be avoided. Fresh or live bait can be preserved for future use by
heading, eviscerating, brining, and icing or freezing.

Herring cut spinners are shaped fillets from 8- to 10-inch herring
and are a very effective bait.

## TROLLING

While the trolling tactic is quite similar to the motor mooching technique mentioned previously, there are some basic gear and technique differences. Basically, trolling requires the use of heavier gear than motor mooching. At times, attracting devices such as dodgers or rotating flashers are
used with either bait or lures. Trolling is accomplished by towing gear
through the water at slow speed by use of one of several methods of propul-
sion--rowing, sail, or power.

Use of the simplest trolling gear is technically classified as motor
mooching and is dealt with under mooching. The simple trolling set-up utilizes the same basic tackle but exchanges bait for a spinner, spoon, fly,
or plug lure. In many cases, the slip sinker replaces the banana-shaped
mooching sinker to allow more distance between sinker and lure for better
lure action.

The fact is, trolling is a very effective method of taking salmon.
Since chinook salmon are seldom found near the surface, in most waters it
is necessary to use a lead weight sufficient to take the lure to the desired depth--hence, the use of gear that would usually be considered much
heavier than warranted by the average salmon landed.

A more complicated technique adds the use of a dodger. The technique employs a slow troll which causes the dodger to flutter and cause movement of a bait or lure. While a plug can be used, it does not produce well as dodger and lure counteract each other. On the other hand, flies, artificial squid-type lures, some spoons, and certain bait hook-ups are given an enhancing darting movement by the wobbling dodger. Several things should be considered in using this trolling technique, but most important are troll speeds and the increased drag of the tackle.

Fishing a dodger or flasher properly calls for gear that is now pretty much standard. A fairly heavy fiberglass or split bamboo rod of from 6 to 8 feet long for dodger, and 9 to 10 feet long for flasher and capable of handling 32 ounces of lead is a necessity. Several manufacturers produce adequate star-drag reels suited for the task of "giving" line smoothly at a preset pressure without freezing up from overheating. Generally, single-action reels made for wire line fishing are used with flasher gear.

Braided wire and monel lines are becoming very popular due, in short, to their faster sinking and low drag qualities. The advantages are obvious, but monofilament is still used.

The dodgers and flashers (Figure 6) vary in size and, as mentioned, are fish-attracting devices which also provide the action for the lure or bait.

Terminal gears (Figure 6) are the same for both dodgers and flashers and include polar bear hair flies, spoons, plastic squid lures, and various herring baits.

The troll speed should be just fast enough to cause the dodger to flutter. Too much speed will cause it to rotate and should prove much less productive. Even at the slow speeds recommended, the additional hardware will

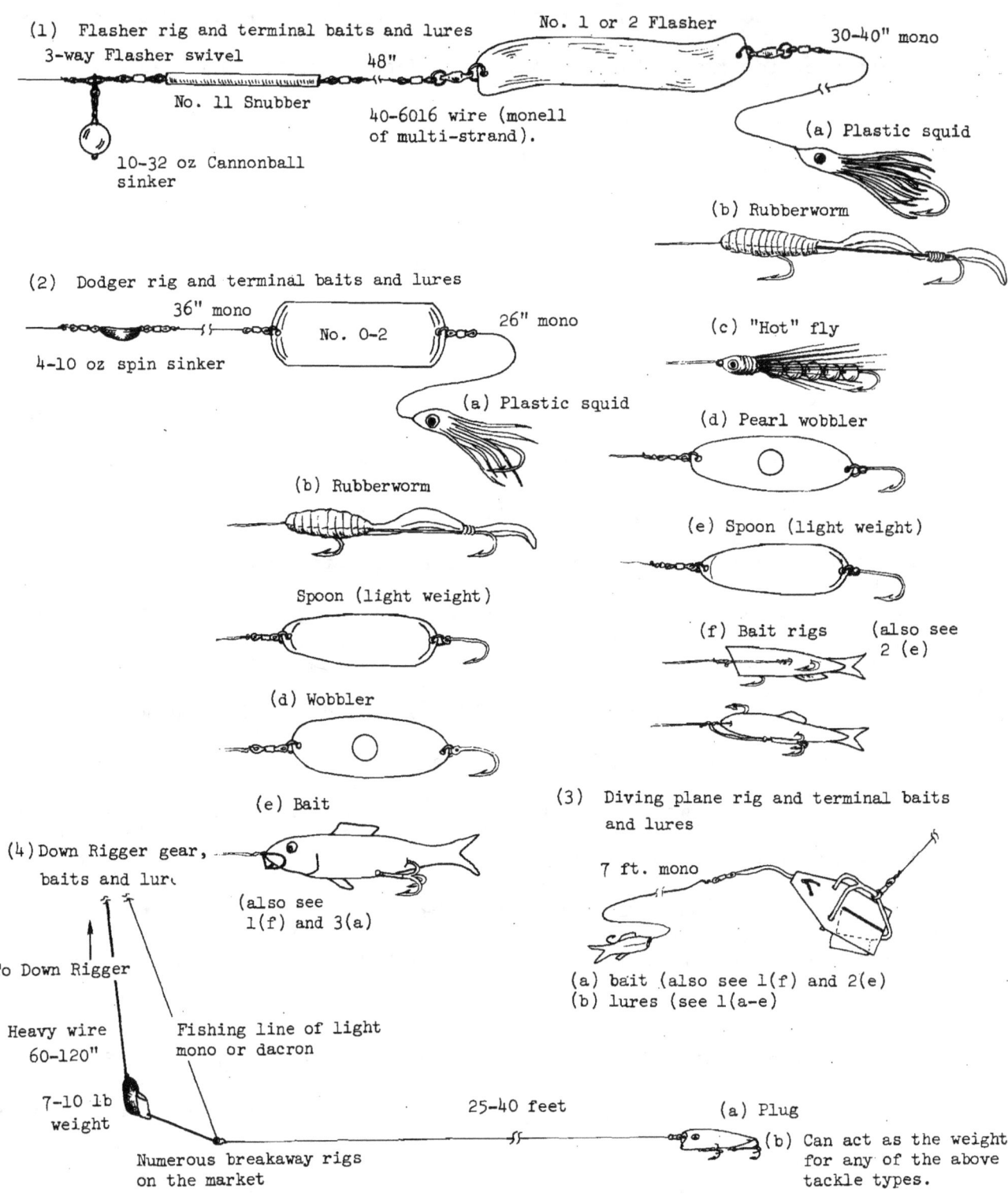

(1) Flasher rig and terminal baits and lures
3-way Flasher swivel          48"          No. 1 or 2 Flasher          30-40" mono
No. 11 Snubber          40-6016 wire (monell of multi-strand).
10-32 oz Cannonball sinker
(a) Plastic squid
(b) Rubberworm

(2) Dodger rig and terminal baits and lures
36" mono          No. 0-2          26" mono
4-10 oz spin sinker
(a) Plastic squid
(b) Rubberworm
Spoon (light weight)
(d) Wobbler
(e) Bait

(c) "Hot" fly
(d) Pearl wobbler
(e) Spoon (light weight)
(f) Bait rigs          (also see 2 (e)

(3) Diving plane rig and terminal baits and lures
7 ft. mono
(a) bait (also see 1(f) and 2(e)
(b) lures (see 1(a-e)

(4) Down Rigger gear, baits and lures
(also see 1(f) and 3(a)
To Down Rigger
Heavy wire 60-120"
7-10 lb weight
Fishing line of light mono or dacron
Numerous breakaway rigs on the market
25-40 feet
(a) Plug
(b) Can act as the weight for any of the above tackle types.

Figure 6.--Salmon sport troll gear and terminal rigs.

create a lot more stress than light gear recommended for mooching will handle--let alone set the hook and play a fish. Again the question arises--would you tee off with a 9 iron? What I'm getting at is a stiffer rod (both in backbone and tip); a heftier reel and heavier line are required to do a proper job.

More and more of Washington State's salmon faithful have been flocking to the rotating flasher or deep troll ranks. There are some definite benefits to these rigs and the major one is that it puts fish in the boat when used properly. Like every other "sure-fire" gear, there is nothing magic about the rotating flasher. This gear, which utilizes wire lines, heavy weights, a large rotating flasher, and a relatively high trolling speed, allows a fisherman to cover a lot of territory in a short period of time. I would guess that the rotating flasher attracts salmon by simulating the flashing side of a feeding salmon. In any event, a properly working flasher imparts a deadly action to the trailing lure.

As with all angling tactics, the proper rod is one of the keys to success by imparting the desired action while being sensitive enough to proclaim the presence of the smallest caller.

Fishing depth is also of major importance. The rotating flasher tackle allows the angler maximum trolling depth control. The right depth is for the angler to determine. A technique often used is to fish--when practical--gear at different levels until fish are located. There are other methods of getting down to where the fish are and these gears have been described. Admittedly, it doesn't take a purist to consider most deep troll tactics "meat fishing." For those who like to "get 'em in the boat and beat 'em on the head" and have their sport too, various gears have been developed. These include the San Francisco weight release gear, the "break-away" rig, and diving-plane sinker rigs.

Trolling with the use of a device which dives when pulled through the water, known as a diving plane, allows the angler to get to considerable depths without weights, then provides little more drag than the line when a fish is hooked. No flasher or dodger is used, but terminal tackle is the same as mentioned above.

Certain areas have contributed certain specialized gears such as the Tacoma "meat rig" which consists of a "pool cue" rod, wire line, and heavy lead. Terminal gear consists of spoons, spinners, plugs, or a "working" herring bait. In San Francisco, charter boat fishermen get around the effect of a 2-pound weight on a struggling fish by providing a method which allows the weight to fall away when the hooked fish exerts 4-10 pounds of pressure on a spring device. This gear allows the angler to play only the fish but has the drawbacks of loss of the weight and extremely heavy weight tackle for the size of the salmon.

From the Great Lakes-lake trout fishery comes an added innovation which gives the best of both worlds. A wire line is weighted by an 8-pound weight and is attached to "light" angling gear by a "break-away" system, thus allowing for retrieval of the weight after the hooked fish disengages the two lines. The fish is then played on lighter, more sporting gear. This type of gear can incorporate the rotating flasher, making it very versatile while providing maximum sport.

With a few exceptions, plug fishing is an art that went with the old timers of a generation or so ago. An effective method of taking larger mature chinook salmon--or "king," each plug produced had a different action and devotees found that only one in umpteen produced (Bradner, 1969, and Howard, 1947). A modern angler's plug hookup would include either use of the break-awaying or trolling rod, reel, and "mono" line with a slip sinker of 4-20

ounces attached some 20 feet or more above the working plug--the strike
will dislodge the line causing the sinker to slip down to the leader.

Fishing a coho fly requires a rod, reel, "mono" line, and the polar
bear hair lure. The fly is "skipped" in the wake of a fast trolling skiff
for coho salmon.

A light trolling technique developed for coho salmon is fast trolling
a polar bear hair fly. It is necessary that the water conditions be fairly
calm and skies overcast. As a result, most commonly this method is used
in inside waters, such as Puget Sound, and the Inside Passage of Canada
and Alaska. These conditions generally find fish feeding on the surface
and susceptible to this method. The gear used can be a fly rod and reel
or medium action spin or cast gear with 6-10 pound monofilament. Give yourself
some measure of backing (about 300 yards should do) as much larger chinook
will occasionally come to the "party."

LIVE BAIT ANGLING METHODS

Up to now I've mentioned the more significant marine and freshwater
methods of salmon angling. There are some techniques which are not widespread,
such as live bait angling and float fishing from piers or jetties. Each
can be effective.

Live bait angling can be particularly effective where schools of bait
fish have attracted feeding salmon. There are times when fishing "conven-
tional" gears that only prayer will coax a strike, but a live bait will
turn the trick. The tackle is light and weightless, and strikes are "hold
on to your hat" in viciousness. Baits used are whatever is available and
these are generally jigged. The bait is hooked in the back and allowed to
swim about as an injured minnow.

## FRESHWATER ANGLING METHODS

River fishing for salmon requires proper gear for the tactic which includes trolling, drifting, casting, and plunking (Figure 7)--all of which have been described.

River trolling gear is much the same as in the "salt chuck" (a Puget Sound area term for marine estuary) with the exception of terminal gear, which generally consists of diving-type plugs which dive and dart about when pulled or held in current.

Plunking is a shore-bound angler's adaptation of this tactic which employs a weight heavy enough to anchor the rig to one spot in hopes of attracting a migrating salmon.

Drifting, on the other hand, requires light, sensitive gear. Weights are also light (fractions of an ounce usually) so as to present the bait properly in the current and are of the split shot or pencil lead variety. Strikes are generally induced by roe, but spinners, spoons, and bobbers can do the job. Casting a fly or hardware in the form of spoons or spinners is effective on occasion in both salt and fresh water for salmon. While fly casting requires classical fly gear, spinning gear is probably best suited for presenting "hardware."

Salmon are caught in fresh water throughout their range. Salmon are generally thought to stop feeding as they mature and enter freshwater systems to spawn--that is with the notable exception of spring chinook. Even so, methods and gears have been developed that will cause a "non-biter" to take a lure or bait. Briefly, methods for capturing salmon in streams include casting, drifting, plunking, and trolling while trolling and casting are the major lake methods.

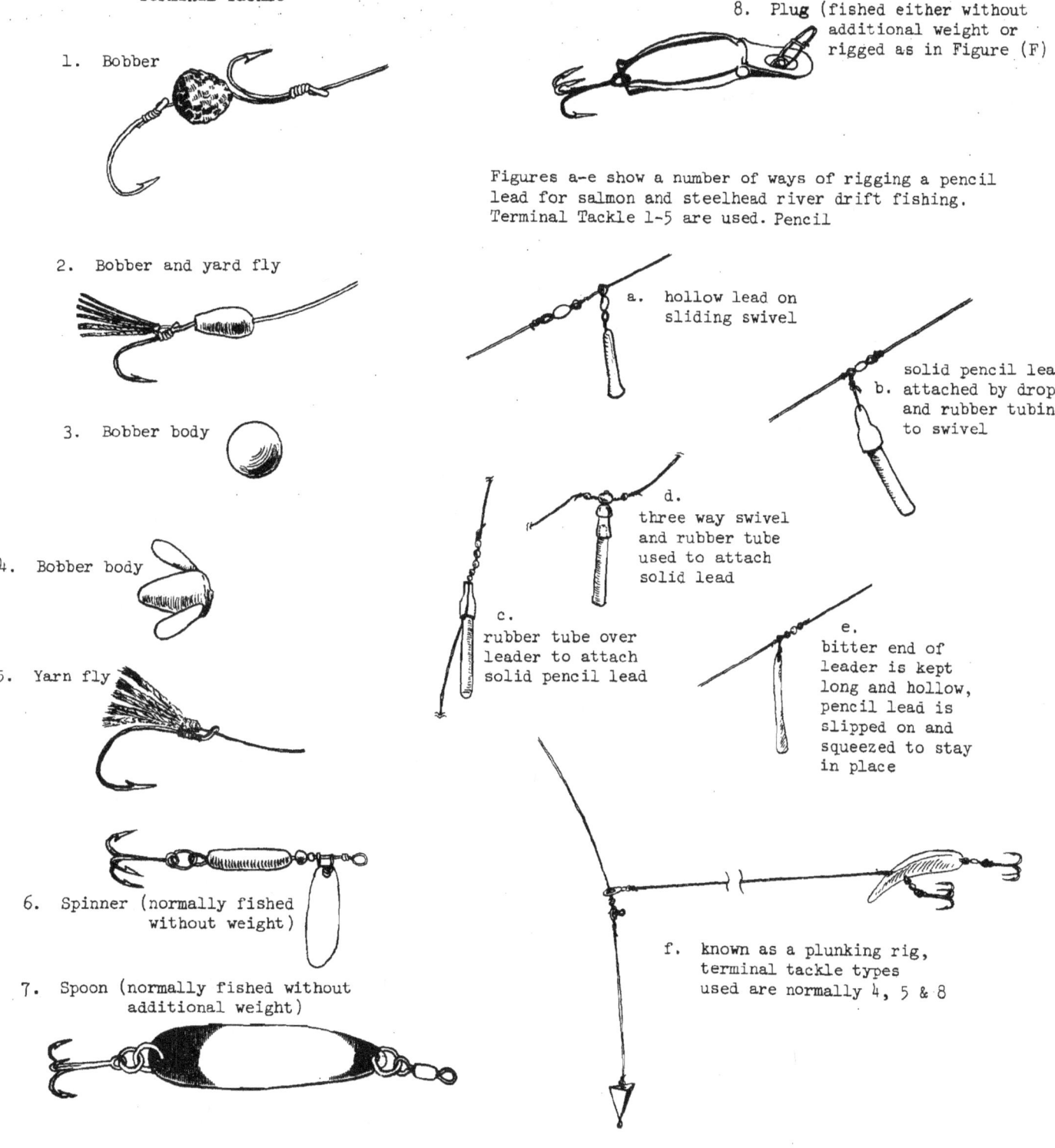

Terminal Tackle

1. Bobber

2. Bobber and yard fly

3. Bobber body

4. Bobber body

5. Yarn fly

6. Spinner (normally fished without weight)

7. Spoon (normally fished without additional weight)

8. Plug (fished either without additional weight or rigged as in Figure (F)

Figures a-e show a number of ways of rigging a pencil lead for salmon and steelhead river drift fishing. Terminal Tackle 1-5 are used. Pencil

a. hollow lead on sliding swivel

b. solid pencil lead attached by dropper and rubber tubing to swivel

d. three way swivel and rubber tube used to attach solid lead

c. rubber tube over leader to attach solid pencil lead

e. bitter end of leader is kept long and hollow, pencil lead is slipped on and squeezed to stay in place

f. known as a plunking rig, terminal tackle types used are normally 4, 5 & 8

Figure 7.--Popular salmon terminal gears and weight rigs for fresh water.

Plunking is one of the more popular methods of bank angling for salmon and is generally a large stream technique. A heavy rod and reel are used to cast a lure and heavy weight out into a known salmon migration channel. The weight is sufficient to anchor a heavy line in deep, heavy current water. Attached via a three-way swivel is the lure (spinners, spoons, bobbers, or plugs), or bait.

Another popular tactic is referred to as "drifting." This light gear technique is simply one in which a bait or lure is cast and allowed to drift along the bottom. Generally, pencil lead or split shot sinkers are used to keep the offering near bottom and slow the drift. Baits, lures, and bait/lure combinations are used. Lures used are in general spoons, spinners, flies, and bobbers, while baits include roe, shrimp, and marine baitfish (Figure 8).

The gear used is light to medium spinning or bait casting. Due to the cast and retrieve techniques involved, this method puts an emphasis on light-weight gear--gear should be as light as the angler's skill and the conditions will allow. Why play with a 5-pound rod/reel and tackle when a 2½-pound rig will do the job? Unlike plunking, where the angler picks his spot and settles in for the day, in drifting the accent is on mobility and the angler should be prepared to fish and hike comfortably--making a good vest and hip boots mandatory. Drifting is also an effective method from a boat.

Casting spinners, spoons, or flies from a riverbank or a boat is also a fish-getter that works in lakes and marine waters. The only difference between this technique and drift fishing is that the lure is retrieved to get a proper action and seldom touches bottom. This method is great in those snaggy tackle-eating stretches or dead water areas where a good drift is impossible.

Trolling for salmon occurs in almost all rivers open to boat angling. While bait is used, generally the lures are chosen from the myriad assortment of diving plugs on the market. In the shallower rivers where depths are 20 feet or less, the plug is attached to the line and no weight is needed to reach the desired depth while deeper waters require the use of a slip sinker attached about 20 feet from the plug.

A unique troll fishery has existed in Washington State's Lake Washington for sockeye salmon (in years when escapement was at acceptable levels)—a species generally regarded as a non-biter due to its food preferences. The factors in successfully angling for sockeye seem to be, first, finding at what depths they are, and second, trolling ever so slowly (small electric motors are gaining in popularity as I've seen larger outboards troll too fast in neutral). The lake sockeye fishery employs strictly lures. Plugs are slow deep trolled in 20 to 80 feet of water by attaching a slip sinker, as described before, while herring dodgers are used to impart a fish-getter action to a wobbling-type spoon and fished at the same depths and speeds.

# LITERATURE CITED

Bradner, E.

    1969. Northwest angling. Binfords and Mort, Publ., Portland, Oreg.,

    239 p.

Haw, F. and R. M. Buckley.

    1973. Saltwater fishing in Washington 2nd edition. Stan Jones Publ.,

    Inc., Seattle, Wash., 198 p.

Haw, F. H. O. Wandler and J. Deschamps.

    1967. Development of Washington State salmon sportfishery through 1964.

    Wash. Dep. Fish., Res. Bull. 7, 192 p.

Howard, H. W.

    1947. Salmon fishing on Puget Sound. Binford and Mort, Publ., Portland,

    Oreg., 122 p.

Squire, J. L.

    1964. Atlas of eastern Pacific Marine game fishing. Fish. and Wildl.

    Ser. BSFW Circ. 174: 8 p. plus 21 charts.